I'm Still SCARED

Also available in the
26 Fairmount Avenue Series

26 Fairmount Avenue
a 2000 Newbery Honor Book

Here We All Are

On My Way

What a Year

Things Will NEVER Be the Same

I'm Still SCARED

written and illustrated by

Tomie dePaola

A 26 FAIRMOUNT AVENUE BOOK

G. P. Putnam's Sons • New York

G. P. PUTNAM'S SONS A division of Penguin Young Readers Group. Published by The Penguin Group. Penguin Group (USA) Inc., 375 Hudson Street, New York, NY 10014, U.S.A. Penguin Group (Canada), 90 Eglinton Avenue East, Suite 700, Toronto, Ontario, Canada M4P 2Y3 (a division of Pearson Penguin Canada Inc.). Penguin Books Ltd, 80 Strand, London WC2R 0RL, England. Penguin Ireland, 25 St. Stephen's Green, Dublin 2, Ireland (a division of Penguin Books Ltd.). Penguin Group (Australia), 250 Camberwell Road, Camberwell, Victoria 3124, Australia (a division of Pearson Australia Group Pty Ltd). Penguin Books India Pvt Ltd, 11 Community Centre, Panchsheel Park, New Delhi - 110 017, India. Penguin Group (NZ), Cnr Airborne and Rosedale Roads, Albany, Auckland 1310, New Zealand (a division of Pearson New Zealand Ltd).Penguin Books (South Africa) (Pty) Ltd, 24 Sturdee Avenue, Rosebank, Johannesburg 2196, South Africa. Penguin Books Ltd, Registered Offices: 80 Strand, London WC2R 0RL, England.

Published simultaneously in Canada. Printed in the United States of America. Book design by Gina DiMassi. Text set in Garth Graphic. Library of Congress Cataloging-in-Publication Data   De Paola, Tomie. I'm still scared / written and illustrated by Tomie dePaola.   p. cm.   — (A 26 Fairmount Avenue book)   1. De Paola, Tomie— Childhood and youth—Juvenile literature. 2. De Paola, Tomie—Homes and haunts— Connecticut—Meriden—Juvenile literature. 3. Authors, American—20th century—Biography—Juvenile literature. 4. Connecticut—Social life and customs— Juvenile literature. 5. World War, 1939-1945—Connecticut—Juvenile literature. 6. Meriden (Conn.)—Biography—Juvenile literature. I. Title: I am still scared. II. Title.   PS3554.E11474Z4754 2006   813'.54—dc22   2005013500   ISBN 0-399-24502-2

13 5 7 9 10 8 6 4 2

First Impression

*For all those who also remember
the terrifying weeks right after
December 7, 1941.*

*On Sunday, December 7, 1941,
the Japanese attacked and destroyed
the United States Pacific Fleet at
Pearl Harbor, on the island of
Oahu in the Hawaiian Islands.
It was a surprise attack.*

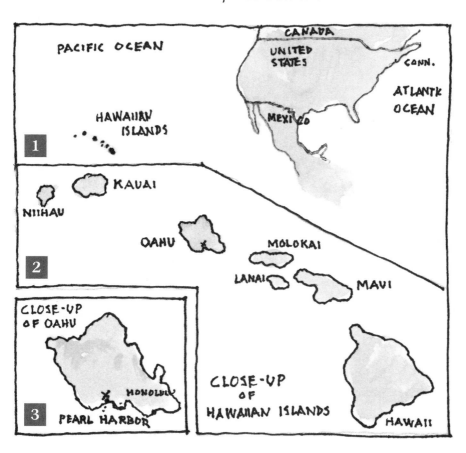

Chapter One

Sunday night. December 7, 1941   very late

Dear Diary,
    I am writing this under the covers.
I am still awake because today was so scary.
Mom said that things will never be the
same.
    I wonder if she is right?
                    Y.B.F.I.T.W.,
BOMBS →   Tomie

"Tomie, Buddy," Mom called. "Get up and get dressed. We have to go to church. Hurry now."

Buddy, my older brother, and I got out of bed, washed up, and got dressed. It was Monday, but we had to go to church. It was a Holy Day. That means that if you're Catholic, like we are, you have to go to church just like on Sunday.

1

"Come on, boys," Dad said. "We have to drop off your baby sister Maureen at the Purcells' before going to St. Joseph's."

The Purcells lived up at the end of Fairmount Avenue. They had a little boy named Jimmy who was just about the same age as Maureen.

The Purcells weren't Catholics, so Mrs. Purcell would watch Maureen while we were at church.

Almost more people were in church than there had been on Sunday. Father O'Connell came down to the altar rail. He was the youngest priest at St. Joseph's in Meriden, Connecticut, where we live. "We will start off this morning by saying the Prayer for Peace," he said. "You will find a copy of the prayer in your pews."

Usually the mass is full of music and candles and smells and bells and quiet. This morning, I heard lots of sniffling, like ladies crying and men clearing their throats. I never heard that before!

The Sisters of Mercy who taught at St. Joseph's School were sitting at the front with all the schoolchildren. Buddy and I went to King Street Public School, so we sat with Mom and Dad.

I saw one of the Sisters pull a white handkerchief out of her sleeve and put it to her eyes. It was like a big flash of lightning because, except for the white stuff around their faces, the Sisters were always dressed in long black dresses and black veils.

Mom, Dad, and Buddy went up to the altar for Holy Communion. I sat quietly in the pew. I hadn't made my First Communion yet.

They came back and knelt down for a little while. Then Mom whispered, "Okay, boys, we have to go now or you'll be late for school."

Because no one had had breakfast, we went into the drugstore across from the church. They had a soda fountain. "We don't have time to go all the way home," Mom said. "So we'll have a quick breakfast here. It will be a treat."

I had a glass of chocolate milk and a doughnut. "From the Vienna Bakery downtown," the lady told me. I had never had a chocolate milk and a doughnut from the Vienna Bakery for breakfast before!

"I need the car, boys, so your mother is going to walk you to school," Dad told us. We said good-bye to Dad and started down Linsley Avenue toward Hanover Street with Mom.

"We'll take the walkway through the cemetery," Mom said. "It comes out on Orange Street, right before King Street."

While we were walking, I saw people standing around, talking quietly.

"What are all those people doing?" I asked.

"Oh, just going to work," Mom said.

It didn't look that way to me.

Mom left Buddy and me at the corner of Orange and King Streets. That's where the school was.

"I'm going to take the bus home. Be good, boys," Mom said, kissing us.

When Buddy and I got to school, I saw the two teachers who were on duty in the upper school yard with the two teachers from the lower school yard. They were talking in low voices. I couldn't hear what they were saying.

The older kids were talking in groups, too. Buddy went over to his sixth-grade friends. I looked around. There was my best friend, Jeannie.

"What's everyone talking about?" I asked her.

"I guess it's all about the attack on Pearl Harbor yesterday," Jeannie said.

"My mom said that things will never be the same," I told Jeannie.

"My father and Mr. Conroy were talking this morning about how there will probably be a war," Jeannie said. "They didn't know I heard them."

"My uncle Charles said the same thing yesterday," I said. "He and his girlfriend, Viva, his best friend, Mickey Lynch, and my grandparents, Tom and Nana, came up to our house. I heard Mom on the phone saying that we need to be together."

"I don't know why nobody will tell us anything," Jeannie said.

"Buddy said that we're just kids," I said. "He may be older, but he's just a kid, too," I added.

Then the school bell rang.

Chapter Two

It was time to go inside. All the kids lined up by class. One by one, we filed into the school and down the hall or up the stairs to our rooms.

Miss Burke, the principal, was usually standing in front of her office, watching us come into the school. Today she wasn't there. We could hear her in her office, talking on the telephone.

We had to take our coats and stuff off before going into the classroom. In first grade we had a coatroom in the back of our classroom. But in second grade we had to use a small space next to the stairway leading down to the auditorium.

It was always a pain in the winter. We had so many coats to hang up and galoshes (or Arctics, as we called the rubber boots we wore to keep our shoes dry) to take off and put away.

School was always smelly in the winter, especially if it was snowing.

"Wet wool," Jack Rule told us. "My grandma says winter clothes are made from wool and when they get wet, they smell." Well, Jack's grandma was right. On a snowy day, the whole school had a "wet wool" smell.

Then there was the "mittens drying on the radiators" smell. It was even worse than "wet wool." It was Miss Luby's bright idea. She was the school nurse. After recess our mittens were always soaking wet from making snowmen and snowballs. Miss Luby said that they had to be dry before we could put them on to go home. "Wet mittens will give you a cold," she said.

So, since the radiators in each room were hot, we lined up our mittens on the tops, just like hot dogs on a grill at a picnic.

The steam from the wet mittens would

start rising as they dried. The classroom got hotter. The windows dripped. The smell got stronger.

Now we had a second winter smell—the "hot wool mittens" smell. It was even stinkier than the plain "wet wool" smell.

But today no one was thinking about mittens.

Suddenly, the door to our classroom opened. It was the school secretary, Miss Philomena.

"Boys and girls," she said, "we are going to have a school assembly. When the bell rings, go to the auditorium exactly the way Miss Gardner has taught you." Miss Philomena and Miss Gardner whispered to each

other, and Miss Philomena left. Why did they always whisper? The teachers didn't want us to hear stuff. Why?

Jeannie and I looked at each other. What was going on?

Chapter Three

"Boys and girls," Miss Gardner said. "When the bell rings, line up in order. Then, we will go down to the auditorium when our turn comes."

The bell rang. We got in line. Miss Gardner opened the door and waited as kids from the upper floor of the school filed by on the way to the auditorium. Sixth-graders, fifth-graders, fourth-graders.

Next Miss Fisher's combination second and third grade went by. Then we went, followed by the first-graders. The kindergartners stayed in their room.

We went down the staircase

with "NO TALKING" until we came to the door to the auditorium. It was also the gym.

Mr. Walters, the janitor, had opened up the big wooden doors that separated the gym part from the auditorium. All the seats, made up of six wooden folding chairs connected to each other, were set up in rows, filling the whole room.

This was serious.

The teachers helped us get settled in our chairs.

Miss Burke walked up onto the stage. She always wore purple. Today she looked very stern.

"Students, please all rise." A sixth-grade boy came up on the stage holding the flag.

"We will now say the Pledge of Allegiance to the flag." We did.

"You may now sit. Yesterday, as many of you know, a terrible thing happened at Pearl

Harbor. It is in Hawaii. Our entire Pacific Fleet of ships is based there. Even though it is far away from here, it affects us as well. Later, at noontime, President Roosevelt will talk to the American people over the radio. Mr. Brown, the superintendent of schools, has informed us that we are closing the schools early so you can be at home with your families when the president speaks.

"I want you all to go right home. Older children, if you have a younger brother or sister, be sure to see that you take him or her home safely. We'll see you all back here tomorrow when school will be in session, as usual."

Buddy came down to Miss Gardner's room to walk me home. Jeannie lives just around the corner from our house, so she came with us.

When we got home, Mom was surprised to see us. She was in the kitchen with Maureen.

"School got out early," Buddy said.

"So we could hear the president on the radio," I added.

"That's good," Mom said. "Your dad is coming home to hear the president, too. I'm fixing cream of tomato soup and grilled cheese sandwiches for lunch. We'll eat as soon as he gets here."

We heard Dad's car pull into the driveway. Dad came in, kissed Mom and Maureen, patted Buddy on the shoulder, and mussed up my hair.

We all sat down at the kitchen table and ate our lunch. Dad got up and turned on the radio in the living room as Buddy and I helped clear the table.

Then we all gathered around the radio.

"The president is going to talk to a joint session of Congress," Mom told Buddy and me. I wasn't sure what that was. But I knew it was important.

"Here we go," Dad said.

"Ladies and gentlemen," the announcer said, "the President of the United States, Franklin Delano Roosevelt."

Chapter Four

Monday, December 8, 1941

Dear Diary,
   Today we listened to President Roosevelt on the radio from Washington, D. C.
He asked the Congress to say to the world that our country is now at war because of the bombing at Pearl Harbor.
   At 4:00 P.M. the Congress met in the Capitol Building and declared WAR.
   I've never been in a war before.
             Y. B. F. I. T. W. ,
              Tomie

Right after President Roosevelt spoke on the radio, the phone started to ring. All the relatives were calling.

Mom and Dad decided that we should go down to Wallingford to see Nana and Tom and Uncle Charles.

When we got there, my grandfather, Tom,

and Uncle Charles were still at Tom's grocery store.

"You children stay in the parlor and play with the blocks. Buddy, get them out of the sewing room. I have to talk with your mother and father," Nana said. She took them right into the kitchen.

Buddy, Maureen, and I were building things with the blocks when Tom and Uncle Charles, his girlfriend, Viva, and his best friend, Mickey Lynch, came in. They said hello and went into the kitchen. I could hear talking. Then it sounded like someone was crying.

Tom came into the parlor. "Well, kids," he said, "how is everything going? Shall we play a game of Chinese checkers?"

I went into the sewing room and got the Chinese checkers board and the bag of marbles that were used to play the game. Tom had taught me how to play last year. I loved it. I was better at it than Buddy. But today I couldn't pay attention.

"Hey, Timothy," Tom said. (My grandfather called me Timothy for a nickname.) "That's the third bad move you've made. What's the matter?"

"I'm scared," I said.

"Oh, Timothy, me bucko," Tom said as he sat down and pulled me up into his lap. "You don't have to be scared. You'll see, everything will be all right. You have to be brave."

"How come all the grown-ups are whispering and whenever we little kids come into the room, they all stop talking?" I asked Tom.

"Well," Tom said, "I think that some grown-ups just don't want to frighten all you kids. War is pretty scary, so they are just trying to protect you."

I was beginning to feel a little better.

"Will we all be killed?" I whispered.

"Oh, I don't think so," Tom said. "You know, Nana and I, your mom, and Uncle Charles went through the First World War and look at us. We're still here. It will be okay. I'll make sure of it."

I really felt better now. I knew that I had the best grandfather in the world.

"Come into the kitchen, children," Nana called. "Have some soup."

The grown-ups were sitting around the big kitchen table. Viva was drying her eyes. Mom and

Nana put out three bowls of homemade vegetable soup. The grown-ups weren't eating.

We had apple pie for dessert.

"Boys," Mom said, "Uncle Charles wants to tell you something."

"Buddy, Tomie," Uncle Charles said, smiling at us, "I've joined the Army. I'm going to be a soldier and fight in the war." Viva started to cry again.

Chapter Five

Tuesday, December 9, 1941

Dear Diary,
  School was really different today.
We had another assembly. Miss Burke
told us that we were at war, but
school wouldn't change.
  Then we sang "My Country 'Tis of
Thee" and we went back to our
classrooms.
                  Y. B, F, I, T, W,
                    Tomie

Once we were back in our classroom, Miss Gardner told us that today we would have our very first music lesson. The music supervisor was Mr. Conklin. He was like Mrs. Bowers, the art supervisor. He would come to King Street School every couple of months or so, and class by class, we would go up to the music room. It was on the second floor of the old part of the school. The music room was a classroom with rows of the same kind of seats that were in the auditorium. There was a blackboard and a piano.

Miss Mulligan, the fifth-grade teacher, played the piano in the auditorium for our assemblies. She played the piano for Mr. Conklin and our music lessons. The other teachers watched Miss Mulligan's class while she was off in the music room.

It was our turn. We lined up—as usual— and walked to the music room as quietly as we could. We didn't want to disturb the other classes.

Miss Gardner went to take care of Miss Mulligan's class. Our music lesson began.

Mr. Conklin had this funny-looking thing in his hand. It was made out of a wooden piece with five wires sticking out of it. Pieces of chalk would fit at the end of the wires.

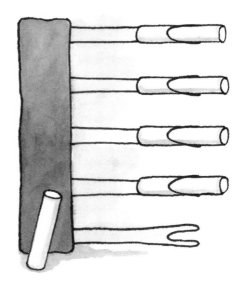

Mr. Conklin drew on the blackboard with the "thing." There were five white lines evenly spaced on the blackboard.

"This is called a staff," Mr. Conklin said. "It holds all the notes. Miss Mulligan, if you please . . ."

Miss Mulligan began to play one note at a time and Mr. Conklin sang the notes "DO, RE, MI." As he sang, he drew small notes on the lines and the spaces of the staff. "These eight notes make up all the music we will sing this year. Now let's try it together."

We all sang, "DO, RE, MI, FA, SOL, LA, TI, DO." It was called "the scale." We went up the scale and down the scale.

"Very, very good, boys and girls," Mr. Conklin said. Then he passed out songbooks. We opened them up and on the first page was "My Country 'Tis of Thee." We sang it again. Miss Mulligan told Mr. Conklin that we had sung it at the assembly this morning.

"We can never sing it enough," Mr. Conklin said. "All right, boys and girls, now we will start to learn another patriotic song, 'America the Beautiful.'"

Mr. Conklin drew another scale on the blackboard. Then, one by one, he drew the notes on the scale and Miss Mulligan played them on the piano.

"Now follow along with your songbooks," Mr. Conklin said. We did. It was fun. Before you knew it, we were singing the first lines, "O beautiful for spacious skies, / For amber waves of grain."

"That's it for today," Mr. Conklin said. "Next, I will test everyone's voice, one at a time."

One by one, we went into the Teachers'  Room. We had to sing something for Mr. Conklin. When my turn came, I sang, "I Ain't Afraid of a Policeman." It was the song I sang when I was the pirate in Miss Leah's dance recital in the spring. It was also the song I sang on the record my grandfather, Tom, and I made at the Savin Rock Amusement Park.

"You have very good pitch, young man," Mr. Conklin said. "We'll have to see if we can give you some solos." That meant I would get to sing something all by myself. It was a very exciting morning.

During recess, Jeannie told me that Mr. Conklin had said she had a good voice, too. Maybe we'd get to sing a DUET! That's when two people sing together. We were so busy talking about our music lesson that we forgot all about the war.

Chapter Six

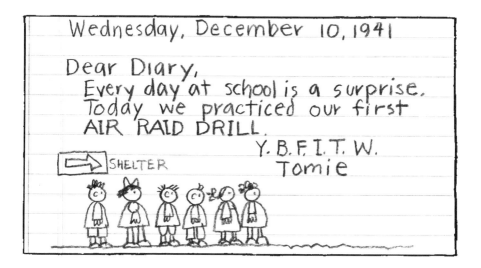

Wednesday, December 10, 1941

Dear Diary,
Every day at school is a surprise.
Today we practiced our first
AIR RAID DRILL.
                    Y. B. F. I. T. W.
SHELTER   Tomie

Today in school, after we said the Pledge of Allegiance to the flag and sang "My Country 'Tis of Thee," Miss Gardner told us to sit down with our hands folded on our desks. She had an important announcement to make.

"This morning we will have our first AIR RAID DRILL. You all know what a FIRE DRILL is."

A FIRE DRILL was when the bell rang and the fire alarm went off. The fire alarm was like a horn sound. All the classes lined up quickly and filed out of the school building. If it was cold, we put on our coats first. We had to stand away from the school in a special spot for each class. The teacher had her attendance book with her. She checked to make sure every student was there.

Miss Gardner continued, "This morning we received 'Rules for Air Raid Drills' from the Board of Education. Pay attention while I read these rules to you."

I raised my hand.

"What is it, Tommy?" Miss Gardner asked. (In school I had to spell my name T-o-m-m-y instead of T-o-m-i-e.)

"What's an air raid?" I asked.

"Well, I don't think we have to worry about a real air raid. These are the rules just in case there is an air raid. That's why it is called a drill."

I guess Miss Gardner didn't want to explain it to us. It was like Tom told me. Maybe she didn't want to frighten us.

"Now," Miss Gardner said, "here are the rules.

"'When the city air raid siren sounds, the school bell will go off. All the students will leave their classrooms and file down in an orderly manner to the designated shelter area. The students should be able to do this easily, as they are quite used to fire drills.

"'The students will remain in the shelter area until the city's sirens sound the "all clear." The school bell will then ring, signaling that it is safe for the students to return to their classrooms.'"

Miss Gardner had just finished telling us about the air raid drill when the school bell rang. We all lined up at the door behind Miss Gardner.

"Follow me, class," Miss Gardner said. "We are going to the basement."

I had never been to the basement of King Street School before.

We went down the stairs we used to go

to the school yard if there was a fire drill. Today, instead of going outside, we went all the way down the stairs as if we were going to the auditorium. But at the bottom we turned left instead of right. We went along to a dark basement room with just a few lightbulbs in the ceiling.

This was Mr. Walters' furnace room. It had a big coal bin, like the one in Nana and Tom's cellar, and a huge coal furnace. The furnace was hot and glowing.

All along the walls were benches. They

had grade numbers and teachers' names on cards taped to the seat. There we were. "Grade 2—Miss Gardner." We sat down and squeezed close together to make room for everyone.

The rest of the seats were for the kindergarten, the two first grades, Miss Fisher's combination second and third grade, and the other third grade.

The older grades weren't in the furnace room. They were sitting on the floor under the stairs.

The furnace room was dark and spooky.

The furnace made a hissing sound. Some of the little kids began to cry. I don't think they even knew why we all were down here.

I wasn't scared of the dark or the furnace. But I was scared of a real air raid. Was it really going to happen? If so, when? And where were Mom and Dad and Maureen while I was down in the school basement and Buddy was under the stairs?

I needed Mom to explain things to me better.

Chapter Seven

Thursday, December 11, 1941 - before supper

Dear Diary,
   It is so great having a very smart Mom. She explained all about AIR RAIDS - how enemy planes come mostly at night to bomb cities.
   She also told me that it is good to practice for an AIR RAID - just in case. That's what an air raid drill is.
                              Y. B. F. I. T. W.
                                 Tomie

When Buddy and I got home from school, Mom told us that she'd like to talk to both of us.

What did I do? I wondered.

"Here, boys, sit at the kitchen table," Mom said. "I've baked some cookies and I'll get you each a glass of milk."

Our baby sister, Maureen, was sitting in her high chair.

"I talked with your grandfather today, Tomie, and he told me that everything that is happening is making you a little scared. Is that true?"

I nodded yes.

"What about you, Buddy?" Mom asked.

"I'm not scared," Buddy said. "So, can I go out and play with the guys?"

"Well," Mom said, "why don't you just sit and listen. You might be able to help Tomie understand things, and you might have a question or two yourself."

Buddy settled down and grabbed another cookie.

"Okay, Tomie. What do you want to know?" Mom asked.

At first, I didn't know what to say. I wanted to know about everything.

"I asked Miss Gardner what an air raid was and she didn't really tell me. She said she didn't think we had to worry about it. If we don't have to worry about it, how come we are having air raid drills? And what are air raids, anyway?"

Mom put her arm across my shoulder. Then she patiently explained how airplanes were dropping bombs on cities, so they sounded alarms so the people could go and try to be safe in shelters that would protect them from the bombs.

She told us how the Germans, who had started the war in Europe, were dropping bombs every night on London, England. It was called the Blitz. "But the English people are being so, so brave. They have not given in at all," Mom said.

Then she told us that the Japanese were doing the same thing in China.

"And now that we are in the war, we will probably bomb the enemy cities," Mom said sadly. "No one thinks that the Germans can fly clear across the Atlantic Ocean to bomb us, but the government wants everyone to be safe. That's why we will have air raid drills. They are for practice. We will have to practice here at home, too. In the newspaper today, there was a list of things that we'll have to do. So, let me get Maureen out of her high chair and we'll go down to the basement so I can show you where our AIR RAID SHELTER will be."

We went down to the basement. Mom pointed out where she and Dad would fix

up a spot for all of us when we had an air raid drill.

When we got back upstairs, Mom told us that she would have to make curtains out of thick black material to hang on some of the windows of our house. "To keep anyone from seeing our lights," Mom said.

"They are called blackout curtains. Starting on the first of the year, we will have to follow regulations. First, there will be a 'brownout' every night. That means that all unnecessary lights will have to be out in all the houses and stores and even on the streets.

"If there is a blackout drill, then all the lights will have to be out except in the rooms that have blackout curtains on the windows. Then, if there is an air raid drill, all the lights will have to be out and we'll have to go down to the basement."

"I can't remember all that," Buddy said.

"Me, neither!" I chimed in.

"Don't worry, your father and I will remember. There will be separate sirens for all the different drills. And after we practice, you'll see—it'll be easy. And it might even be fun!" Mom said.

I couldn't wait to tell Jeannie, Jack, and some of my other friends at school all about air raid drills, brownouts, and blackout curtains.

Chapter Eight

Saturday, December 13, 1941

Dear Diary,
   Today is Dancing School with
Miss Leah. I love Dancing School.
At regular school, I hate arithmetic.
Miss Gardner says it's very important,
I think reading, spelling, thinking, music,
and, of course, art are important.
   I like Mrs. Bowers, the art teacher,
and Miss Leah the best.
               Y. B. F. I. T. W.
               Tomie

MRS. BOWERS   MISS LEAH   ME

Mom told me that after Dancing School we would go shopping. Dad and Buddy would meet us with Maureen. One of the things we would buy is the material for our blackout curtains. There were four of us in our tap class at Dancing School—Patty Clark, Billy Burns, Carol Morrissey, and me. Miss

Leah had us do our "warm-ups." We did slaps and up-back-downs, drumrolls, paddle turns, and time steps. Then, one by one, we did "traveling steps" from one corner to the other. Mrs. Anderson played the piano for us.

"All right, children," Miss Leah said, "today I am going to start teaching you the tap number you'll do at the recital this coming spring. I already know what I'm going to call it. It will be called 'A Couple of Couples.' The music will be the main song from a new

full-length animated movie that is coming to the Capitol Theatre during the Christmas vacation."

"Is it Mr. Walt Disney's new movie, *Dumbo*?" I asked. "Mom said she'd take me to see it."

"Well," Miss Leah said, "yes, *Dumbo* is coming, too. But this movie was made by the same man who made *Gulliver's Travels* several years ago. It's called *Mr. Bug Goes to Town*. The song is 'We're the Couple in the Castle.' Tomie, you and Billy will learn the words and sing the song together. Carol and Patty will be your partners. Mrs. Anderson doesn't have the music yet. The song is brand-new, but let's start anyway. Now line up in front of the mirror."

This was going to be so much fun.

Miss Leah asked our mothers to take us to see the movie if they could. I knew Mom would certainly take me! Maybe all four of us could go together. That would be great!

After our dancing lesson was over, we met Dad, Buddy, and Maureen at Mr. Frank McLaren's Barber Shop, where Dad worked before he became the State Barber Examiner.

Then we went to Kresge's five- and ten-cent store. They had a fabric department where Mom would buy the thick black material for the blackout curtains.

"You know, Tomie," she told me, "Nana wants a new piece of oilcloth for her kitchen table. Do you want to pick it out?"

I picked out the design with pineapples on it. I hoped Nana would like it.

Next, we went to the Christmas decorations counter. Dad got boxes of icicles and as many Christmas tree lightbulbs as he could. Dad said this probably would be the last Christmas we could buy Christmas tree stuff until the war was over.

We walked a bit, looking at the Christmas decorations in the store windows and at the decorations on all the lampposts.

Dad told us that the mayor's office had said that since the Christmas decorations and lights were already up, they would be lit for several hours every night until New Year's.

Also, people could put up outside decorations on their houses this Christmas. They would be allowed to be lit for several hours until New Year's, too.

"Of course," Dad said, "if there is an air raid drill, all the lights will have to be turned off."

So, we would have the blue lights on the bushes in front of the house and the blue electric candles in the windows. The Christmas tree would be tucked in the corner away from the windows so we could leave it on a little longer every night.

So, I guess we'd have a Christmas pretty much like the ones we had before. But when I went to bed, I thought about the grown-ups and children in England. *What kind of a Christmas would they have?*

Sunday, December 14, 1941

Dear Diary,
   We went to Nana and Tom's house in Wallingford today, just like every Sunday.
   Tom and I listened to "The Shadow" on the radio. Tom asked me if I was feeling better about things. I told him a little bit.
                    Y. B. F. I. T. W.
                       Tomie

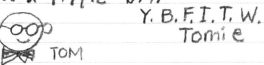
TOM

Monday, December 15, 1941

Dear Diary,
   We started the last week of school before the Christmas vacation. Our class is making paper chains for the hallway decorations. I wish it could be something more exciting.
   Mom has started sewing the blackout curtains.
                    Y. B. F. I. T. W.
                       Tomie

Tuesday, December 16, 1941

Dear Diary,
   Miss Gardner picked me to take
a note upstairs to Miss Early. She teaches
the fourth/fifth grade in the room next to
the music room. I heard a class practicing
Christmas songs for the assembly on
Friday. Our class is not singing anything.
   We put up the paper chains today.
   I wish I could make a wreath
like all the fifth-graders did.
                Y. B. F. I. T. W.
                Tomie

Wednesday, December 17, 1941

Dear Diary,
   Today we got our first report cards.
I had perfect attendance. Miss Gardner
said, "Tommy talks too much and does not
pay attention. He needs work on his
arithmetic, but he is an excellent reader
and speller."
   She also said I enjoyed music and
art. Mom has to sign the report card
and I have to take it back tomorrow.
             Y. B. F. I. T. W.
              Tomie

Report
card
TOMMY
DePAOLA

Chapter Nine

Thursday, December 18, 1941

Dear Diary.
    Bobby B. lost his report card. He had to go to the principal's office. I felt sorry for him. I don't think he did it on purpose.
    I have something to ask Dad when he gets home.
                    Y. B. F. I. T. W.
                      Tomie

MISS BURKE

An older kid in the school yard said that I was an ENEMY because I was Italian and the Italians are fighting the war against us, with the Germans. I told him I was also Irish. He pushed me. I looked for Buddy, but I couldn't find him.

Then I missed my ride home with Jeannie. Her father would pick us up at the corner of Hanover Street and Orange Street. But Mr.

Houdlette wouldn't wait for me if I wasn't right there. He said I "DAWDLED," so I missed the rides home a lot.

Walking home in the winter wasn't much fun. It was cold and sometimes I had to go to the bathroom. If that happened, I'd knock on the door of Mr. and Mrs. Crane's house on Columbus Avenue. Their daughter, Carol, was my best friend before we moved to 26 Fairmount Avenue. Mrs. Crane was always home. She always let me use the bathroom.

Their bathroom was very fancy. It was all green and black tiles. The seat covers on the toilet were green. The Palmolive soap was green. Even the toilet paper was pale green.

Only once, Mrs. Crane wasn't home and—I hate to admit it—I wet my pants. Wet corduroy pants are *not* fun. By the time I got home, my legs were all red and raw. Mom didn't scold me. She just had me take a nice, hot bath and she put clean clothes for me on my bed.

Buddy laughed at me, though. "Just go in the bushes," he said.

Dad finally got home. I asked him if I could ask him something VERY important. I told him what the 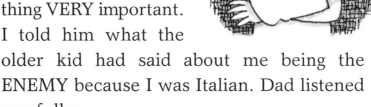 older kid had said about me being the ENEMY because I was Italian. Dad listened carefully.

"Okay, Tomie," he said. "This is what you tell that kid. You are an American. So am I. I was born in Fall River. Nana Fall-River was born in Italy and so was my father. But they came to Massachusetts before I was born in 1907.

"Just because we are of Italian descent—that means our ancestors were Italian—that was a long time ago, and way before Mussolini, the leader of Italy, came into power and decided to join Hitler, the leader of Germany, to fight the war.

"So, don't you worry! I'll tell your brother the same thing. Loads and loads of people here in the United States are genuine Americans, but their ancestors came from other countries—in fact, almost everybody's ancestors came from other places."

See, all I have to do is ask my dad or my mom or Tom. They always tell me the whole truth!

Chapter Ten

Friday, December 19, 1941

Dear Diary,
  We had the Christmas assembly today. Miss Mulligan's class put on a play about THE LITTLE MATCH GIRL. It was sad. The sixth-graders sang Christmas carols. The first-graders recited "The Night Before Christmas." The third and fourth grades did a square dance. All we did was watch.
  School is out for two weeks. Dad is taking me to do my Christmas shopping tonight.
                              Y. B. F. I. T. W.
                                Tomie

ME WATCHING →

The newspaper said that all the stores downtown would be open until 9:00 P.M. every night until Christmas Eve—except Sunday. They are closed every Sunday.

The newspapers had lots of ads about

Christmas shopping. "Don't wait until the last minute," the ads said.

Usually I went downtown with Mom. But today I was going to buy her Christmas present, too, so Dad took me. First, we went into Woolworth's and Kresge's, the two five- and ten-cent stores. I bought Maureen a tiny little doll with "real" hair and arms that moved. Mom would be able to make it lots of clothes.

We went to Bessie Boynton's on Colony Street. We took the elevator to the third floor, where all the Boy Scout stuff was. I bought Buddy a camping kit that had a metal cup that closed up, a metal tube to keep matches from getting wet, and some other stuff. He could wear it on his Boy Scout belt.

We went into Liggett's Drug Store across the street. Dad knew Mac, who worked there.

"Well, hello, young fella!" Mac said to me. "You here to get your grandpa a new pipe?"

For the last three Christmases, I had given Tom a new corncob pipe.

"And here are some pipe cleaners for you, too," Mac said.

Then Dad took me to Upham's Department Store. It was on Colony Street, too.

First I bought two pretty handkerchiefs, one for Nana in Wallingford and the other for Nana Fall-River. I had been in Upham's a lot. I always bought Mom Tweed cologne for her birthday. The lady at the perfume counter knew me.

"Well, hello, Master dePaola"—lots of grown-ups called little boys "Master"—"let me squirt this new cologne in the air for you to smell. Do you want a bottle of Tweed for your mother for Christmas?"

I told her that I was going to buy my mother a pair of nylon stockings for Christmas.

Dad had given me the idea. "Nylon stockings will probably be hard to get because of the war. They need all the nylon thread for parachutes," he had explained.

The stocking counter was right next to the

glove counter. Both counters had tall chairs in front of them. The glove counter had a little cushion on the counter in front of each chair.

"If Madame will put her elbow on the cushion and hold her hand straight up, I will try the glove on for her," the saleslady would say. I loved to watch.

"Little Master dePaola, do you want to try on a glove?" the saleslady asked me once when no one was around. I sat, or rather knelt on the tall chair and put my elbow on the cushion. The saleslady tugged a glove onto my hand, one finger at a time. It was funny.

The stocking counter was different. Stacks and stacks of thin boxes were lined up against

the back wall. Each box had a pair of stockings in it. The nylons were off to one side.
The boxes were arranged by size and color.

"What size and which color?" the saleslady
would ask the customer. If the customer
didn't know the color, the saleslady would get
several boxes off the stack. She'd open one

box at a time, folding
back the tissue paper.
Then she'd carefully put
her hand into the stock-
ing so the customer could
see the color against the
saleslady's skin.

"Here," Dad said.
He handed me a slip of
paper. On it he had
written Mom's size and
the color she liked. I handed it to the
saleslady. She took a flat box off the shelf.

"Would you like to see how pretty your
mommy's legs will look in this color?" she
asked.

"Yes, please," I answered. I wanted to see the nylon stocking on her hand.

Upham's Department Store was great because of two things.

They did free gift wrapping at a special counter. You could pick out the paper and ribbon and watch the lady wrap the box perfectly and make the fanciest bows I had ever seen.

And there were NO cash registers at any of the counters. The salesclerks would put a slip of paper with the price on it and the money in a little metal box. Then they would clip the box onto moving wires that went all over the ceiling of the store. The little box

would end up at the cashier's cage in the back of the store. There, ladies would make the change, put it back in the metal box, and clip it back on the moving wires. In no time at all, it would end up at the counter where it started!

I loved to watch all those little boxes whizzing around the store. It would make a great ride at the Savin Rock Amusement Park.

Chapter Eleven

Saturday, December 20, 1941

Dear Diary,
  Mom is going to put up the blackout curtains when we get back from Miss Leah's Dancing School.
                    Y. B. F. I. T. W.
BLACKOUT   Tomie
   CURTAINS
   →

Mom was busy all week sewing the blackout curtains. She had a "portable Singer sewing machine" that she would put on the dining room table. It was electric and to make it go, you have to press a little lever that fit in a slot on the front with your right leg, just above the knee.

Nana's sewing machine was an old-fashioned "Singer." It was in the "sewing room" under the stairs at her house in Wallingford. It took up more room than Mom's sewing machine. It smelled oily. The way you made it sew was to push with both feet on a metal plate that moved up and down. That made the sewing needle go up and down, too. We kids were not allowed to touch either sewing machine.

"You could sew the needle right through your finger, if you don't know how to work it," Nana always warned.

After a week, there was a pile of black curtains all ready to hang on the windows of the rooms of the first floor and even the little windows at the top of the walls in the basement.

Dad said, "Every house in Meriden and Wallingford has to have blackout curtains. Maybe in all of Connecticut. Maybe in the whole country."

I was disappointed that the bedrooms, especially the bedroom I shared with Buddy, wouldn't have blackout curtains.

"What if I turn the light on—by mistake," I said.

"Oh, I'll bet you won't," Mom said, smiling.

So, the blackout curtains were all ready.

They had to be put up so NO light would show out the windows at night.

"We'll have to close them every night before we turn the lights on. That way, enemy

airplanes won't see anything from way up,"
Mom said. "They won't even know Meriden
is here."

"If they ever come here," I said, a little
worried again.

"That's right, Tomie. If they EVER come
here," Mom said. "Now let's get the bus so
we can go to Miss Leah's."

On the bus to Dancing School, I heard
some grown-ups talking.

"All this fuss," the lady said. "I had to sew
and sew and sew those silly blackout curtains. What would enemy planes care about
Meriden for?"

"Well," the other lady said, "we have some important factories here. Why, I understand that every ball bearing that is being used in all the war equipment is made right here in Meriden."

"Is that true?" I whispered to Mom.

"I suppose so," she said. "The New Departure factory makes ball bearings. You should ask your father tonight when he gets home from work."

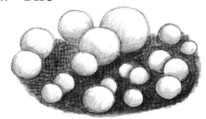

My dad was the State Barber Examiner for the state of Connecticut. His office was in the State Office Building in Hartford, Connecticut. It was right near the State Capitol building.

Buddy and I had visited Dad's office a couple of times.

Dad had an assistant called Joe Suma. Their job was to visit the barbershops in Connecticut to make sure they were clean. Barbershops were supposed to follow "Health Rules." One important rule was that barbershops had to have a big jar of blue liquid to

keep all the combs in. It was called a "SANITIZER." It killed germs and stuff.

"If you don't see a sanitizer on the barber's counter," Dad told us, "don't go in. You might get cooties from a dirty comb."

I thought Dad's job was very important.

There were two ladies in Dad's office, too. They were the secretaries. My favorite was Miss Monica Schwartz. One time she gave me some stationery with Dad's name on it. I was very impressed. I took it to school, but Miss Gardner just looked at it and said, "That's nice. Now get back to your arithmetic."

We knew Miss Monica Schwartz pretty well. She was Joe Suma's girlfriend. She had us call her by her nickname, "Monnie." Monnie and Joe were from Waterbury. It was near Meriden.

Monnie and Joe came to our house for hot dog roasts and parties all the time. Monnie could do somersaults. Dad took home movies of her. She was a favorite of us kids.

As soon as Dad walked in the door, I asked him about the ball bearings.

"Dad, is it true that all the ball bearings used in the war stuff are made right here in Meriden?"

"That's true, Tomie. And guess what? I'm going to be working at New Departure," Dad said.

"What about inspecting all the barber-shops?" Buddy asked.

"I'll still go to Hartford every day Monday through Friday. I'll be working at the factory at night."

Dad told us that all the state workers were being asked to take "war jobs" along with their other jobs.

"How are you going to do that?" Buddy asked.

"After New Year's, I'll still be working in my office just like I do now, but not all day. I'll be working at New Departure as a 'foreman.' That means I'll make sure everyone's doing their job. I'll be working what they call the 'graveyard shift' from midnight until eight-thirty in the morning."

"When will you sleep?" I asked.

Dad said that he would get home from Hartford around three in the afternoon and go to bed and sleep until eleven at night. Then he would go to New Departure to work until eight-thirty in the morning, come home, have breakfast, clean up, and then go back to his office in Hartford.

"I won't get to see as much of you as I do now," Dad said, "except on weekends."

And he was right.

For the whole war, we never saw Dad except on Saturdays and Sundays. When we got home from school, he was asleep. Then he left for work when we were asleep. Dad was always either "upstairs asleep" or "at work."

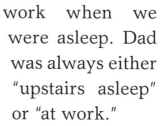

Sunday, December 21, 1941

Dear Diary,
　We went down to Wallingford like we do every Sunday. Tom and I listened to "The Shadow" and "One Man's Family" on the radio.
　Tomorrow we will put up the Christmas tree.
　　Y.B.F.I.T.W.
　　Tomie

Monday, December 22, 1941

Dear Diary,
　Our Christmas tree is up. Dad said to save the boxes for the ICICLES so we can use them again next year. Mom and Dad are going to have an OPEN HOUSE party again this year.
　I hope I can stay up for a little while, now that I am in second grade.
　　Y.B.F.I.T.W.
　　Tomie

3 DAYS 'TIL CHRISTMAS

Tuesday, December 23, 1941

Dear Diary,
   Mom is going to help me wrap my Christmas presents. My present for Mom was gift wrapped at Upham's.
   Last night Mom let me listen to the LUX RADIO THEATER on the radio because it is school vacation.
   LUX RADIO THEATER is on at nine o'clock at night.
                    Y. B. F. I. T. W.
                       Tomie

Chapter Twelve

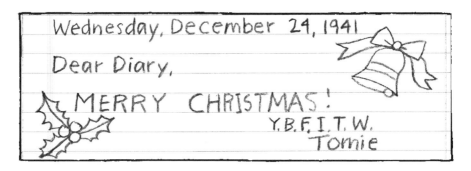

Wednesday, December 24, 1941

Dear Diary,

MERRY CHRISTMAS!
Y.B.F.I.T.W.
Tomie

Well, even though we were at war, Christmas was great. We had a beautiful tree.

Mom and Dad's Christmas Eve Party was crowded with people that I know: Uncle Charles and his girlfriend, Viva; Mickey Lynch; Vinnie (from Wallingford, too) and his girlfriend, Queenie; Monnie and Joe; our cousin Helen and her husband, Carl, who is a soldier; Cousin Mabel and her husband, Bill Powers; Mr. and Mrs. Nadile; Mr. and Mrs. Houdlette; the Conroys; and all the neighbors and friends from all over Meriden and Wallingford.

The next morning Buddy, Maureen, and

I got up very early. We wanted to see what Santa Claus had brought us. We got lots of things, including a big swing and seesaw set for the backyard.

We had Christmas dinner in Wallingford at Nana and Tom's. Nana gave me a new diary for 1942. She and Tom gave Buddy and me a small radio for our bedroom.

On the way home, Dad decided to drive around a little so we could see people's Christmas decorations and lights.

"We may not see this for a while," he said.

Because of the war, I thought.

When we got home, we turned on the outside lights on the bushes, the electric candles in the windows, and the Christmas tree. We were allowed to have outside Christmas

lights on for a few hours each night during Christmastime.

Two days later, Mom took Jeannie and me to see Mr. Walt Disney's brand-new movie, *Dumbo*. It was about a little elephant who had big ears and could fly. It was excellent although Mrs. Jumbo, Dumbo's mother, got put in jail for spanking some mean boys that made fun of Dumbo's ears. I liked the part where Mrs. Jumbo puts her trunk out of the barred windows and Dumbo crawls onto it. Then Mrs. Jumbo sings a lullaby. It was so sad.

Mr. Walt Disney really knows how to make very good cartoon movies.

A few days later, Mom and I met Carol Morrissey and her mom at the Capitol Theatre to see *Mr. Bug Goes to Town*. That was the movie Miss Leah wanted us to see. It was all about these bugs that lived in an empty lot right near Broadway in New York City. The hero was a grasshopper named Hoppity. His girlfriend was a honeybee.

The main song was "We're the Couple in the Castle." That was the song that Billy Burns and I would sing to our partners, Patty Clark and Carol Morrissey. *Gosh,* I thought, *will we boys be GRASSHOPPERS and the girls BEES?*

Even though it wasn't by Mr. Walt Disney, it was a really good movie, too. The movies were a Double Feature, so we settled down to wait for the second movie, then the newsreel started. It was filled with scenes of burning buildings in London, England, explosions everywhere, and air raid sirens blasting out. Mom and Mrs. Morrissey quickly took Carol and me out to the lobby.

Mom put her arm around me and whispered, "I'm sorry. I didn't want you to see that!"

Carol's mother was talking quietly to her, too. Carol and I looked at each other. I was

afraid I would not be able to sleep at night. I was afraid I'd have nightmares about all those destroyed buildings and all the hurt people.

It was the first time I actually saw WAR, even though it was only in the movies.

Wednesday. December 31, 1941

Dear Diary,
   Well, the year is almost over- just a few more hours. Last year no one thought we'd be in a World War.
   Mom and Dad are having a party, though. Mom made lots of things to eat. She made celery sticks with pink cream cheese on them. I helped. This may be the last party that Uncle Charles and his girlfriend, Viva, will be at together for a while. Uncle Charles will wear his Army uniform. Buddy is going to wear his Boy Scout uniform. I'll be allowed to stay up for a while.
   I heard Mom say on the phone to Nana. "I think Tomie is doing better with everything that is going on."
   But dear Diary, even though I feel better, I'm still scared!
                              Y.B.F.I.T.W.
                                 Tomie

The End

26

Franklin D. Roosevelt's Pearl Harbor Speech, December 8, 1941

Mr. Vice President, Mr. Speaker, Members of the Senate, and of the House of Representatives:

Yesterday, December 7th, 1941—a date which will live in infamy—the United States of America was suddenly and deliberately attacked by naval and air forces of the Empire of Japan.

The United States was at peace with that nation and, at the solicitation of Japan, was still in conversation with its government and its emperor looking toward the maintenance of peace in the Pacific.

Indeed, one hour after Japanese air squadrons had commenced bombing in the American island of Oahu, the Japanese ambassador to the United States and his colleagues delivered to our Secretary of State a formal reply to a recent American message. And while this reply stated that it seemed useless to continue the existing diplomatic negotiations, it contained no threat or hint of war or of armed attack.

It will be recorded that the distance of Hawaii from Japan makes it obvious that the attack was *deliberately planned many days or even weeks ago. During the intervening time, the Japanese government has deliberately sought to deceive the United States by false statements and expressions of hope for continued peace.*

The attack yesterday on the Hawaiian Islands has caused severe damage to American naval and military forces. I regret to tell you that very many American lives have been lost. In addition, American ships have been reported torpedoed on the high seas between San Francisco and Honolulu.

Yesterday, the Japanese government also launched an attack against Malaya.

Last night, Japanese forces attacked Hong Kong.

Last night, Japanese forces attacked Guam.

Last night, Japanese forces attacked the Philippine Islands.

Last night, the Japanese attacked Wake Island.

And this morning, the Japanese attacked Midway Island.

Japan has, therefore, undertaken a surprise offensive extending throughout the Pacific area. The facts of yesterday and today speak for themselves. The people of the United States have already formed their opinions and well understand the implications to the very life and safety of our nation.

As commander in chief of the Army and Navy, I have directed that all measures be taken for our defense. But always will our whole nation remember the character of the onslaught against us.

No matter how long it may take us to overcome this premeditated invasion, the American people in their righteous might will win through to absolute victory.

I believe that I interpret the will of the Congress and of the people when I assert that we will not only defend ourselves to the uttermost, but will make it very certain that this form of treachery shall never again endanger us.

Hostilities exist. There is no blinking at the fact that our people, our territory, and our interests are in grave danger.

With confidence in our armed forces, with the unbounding determination of our people, we will gain the inevitable triumph—so help us God.

I ask that the Congress declare that since the unprovoked and dastardly attack by Japan on Sunday, December 7th, 1941, a state of war has existed between the United States and the Japanese empire.

A Note from the Author

Over the years, letters from my young readers have increasingly asked, "When are you going to write a chapter book?" But the idea seemed daunting. Then one day, my longtime assistant, Bob Hechtel, made a suggestion. "Why don't you write about all the things that you talk about from your childhood, but can't put in a single picture book?" DING—the bell went off—the lightbulb lit. And here I am, six books and seven years later.

From the beginning, it wasn't hard for me to conjure up all the clear memories I have (and have had for years) of my immediate family and all the friends that surrounded me during my growing-up years. And I was fortunate to have those memories reinforced by hours of home movies that my father and mother took from the time I was one year old.

Once I had written *26 Fairmount Avenue*, I knew there was no turning back. But it was particularly interesting for me to find myself back on Sunday, December 7, at the end of *Things Will NEVER Be the Same*. Hearing Roosevelt's voice, seeing the expression on my mother's face, and feeling the uncertainty as if it all happened yesterday: I was in the beginning of "The War Years."

When I began the series back in 1999, I never imagined how timely these later books would become as families today experience the same turmoil and concerns of war that I remember as a little boy. I hope you will find my memories of "The War Years" as moving and vivid as they have been for me.

New Hampshire, 2006

Come home to 26 Fairmount Avenue!

26 Fairmount Avenue
A Newbery Honor Book

"A wonderful introduction to the art of the memoir."
                                    —*The Boston Globe*

★ "Effervescent . . . dePaola seems as at home in this format as he did when he first crossed the threshold of 26 Fairmount Avenue, an address readers will eagerly revisit in the series' subsequent tales."

                        —*Publishers Weekly* (starred review)

Here We All Are

★ "DePaola continues to share engaging childhood memories in this breezy follow-up to *26 Fairmount Avenue*."

                        —*Publishers Weekly* (starred review)

On My Way

★ "DePaola is irresistible."

—*Kirkus Reviews* (starred review)

"DePaola's writing and recollective skills are so fresh that kids will feel like he's sitting right next to them."

—*The Horn Book*

What a Year

"As charming and engaging as its predecessors."

—*Kirkus Reviews*

Things Will NEVER Be the Same

"The fifth installment in the series is delightful."

—*School Library Journal*